a book of clichés

a book of

CLICHÉS

by Joseph W. Valentine

ILLUSTRATIONS BY JAMES L. MACKEY

New York, The Vanguard Press, Inc.

FOREWORD

Weary years ago, before the first Santa Towns, Toylands, and Jungle Villages began to litter the nation's highways, some of us thought fondly of building another sort of wayside haven. There, we felt, the tired traveler might spend a fruitful hour examining a number of objects, seemingly commonplace, that were in fact familiar in a special sense: the ax, for having none to grind; a set of traces, for kicking over; bootstraps, for pulling oneself up by—these and many other exhibits, firmly linked to everyday speech and reading, came to our minds.

As the years passed, the author and his associates managed to build the nucleus of a collection, not without some personal sacrifice.[1] We feel the time is ripe to make our findings known to a wider audience. In the pages that follow, the talents of the artist in our group have created, so to speak, a prospectus of the Cliché Museum as we hope someday to see it.

Granted that anyone wishes to pass through the rich meadows of our language, plucking now and again a bloom from among the myriad weedy clichés that nod there, the choice should initially be limited by basic definition. The French, who gave us the word *clicher* in the first place, have provided this clearly enough. *Clicher* means to produce boiler plate, in the printer's sense; to make a stereotype reproduction from an original— press-ready metal that faithfully duplicates the compositor's hand-set form. Thus, by extension, the word came to mean also any phrase or homily that, through repetition over years—and frequently centuries—has become, as Webster has it, "hack-

[1] There has been some squabbling about how much rope really is enough; also, housing for the ten-foot pole (for not touching things with) finally had to be decided by lot, on a rotating basis. The original lead pipe—a sort of standard meter bar for the measurement of cinches—fortunately remains in its generous donor's custody.

neyed." (The latter splendid cliché, in its turn, derives from horses let to hire; hence, "overworked.")

The selection of clichés to appear in this volume was, of necessity, a subjective process, and many venerable samples of the long-used phrase were culled and cast aside. Some were retained in spite of a paucity of appearances in print; in other cases, voluminous references in the literature of many countries led us well back into antiquity.

Of all the students in this field—a list of those we found most helpful is appended—the late, great Burton Stevenson stands head and shoulders above the rest. His scholarship, patience, and omnivorous curiosity are beyond compare, and his stature is such that any praise here will scarcely serve to increase it.

To cite a case history of a cliché where background material is virtually lacking, let us examine "caught with your pants down," certainly a familiar enough phrase. The image is obvious, whether one chooses the sexual or the scatological context. Historically, it cannot antedate the invention of tailored clothing— roughly attributable to the peoples of Central Asia in the second or first millennium B.C.—since you cannot take down what you do not have. Here, even the redoubtable Stevenson stands mum: "Keep your pants on," he has; "scare the pants off," yes; "to have ants in your pants" proves to be far from modern slang; but where is "caught with pants down"?

The record shows this cliché's appearance in print only quite recently in magazines and novels, but surely it must have been used in this country at least a century ago. Charles Funk, another skilled harvester among the weeds, thinks that the phrase arose from the predicament of American frontiersmen faced with the call of nature in a forest filled with hostile Indians. The author and his associates prefer an Elizabethan (or other) boudoir connotation. But neither side has proof for his preference. We will appreciate receiving documented source material if any reader can provide it.[2]

At quite the other end of this spectrum stands "calling a spade a spade." This has been a popular pastime, the record shows, for substantially more than two thousand years, despite some curious transformations. Mark Twain freshened up the phrase in his 1908 account of a conversation with Elinor Glyn: "I talked with her," he wrote, "with daring frankness, frequently calling a spade a spade instead of coldly symbolizing it as a snow shovel." The melancholist Robert Burton, in 1621, boasted, "A loose, plain, rude writer, I shall call a spade a spade"; and the elegant Cicero, some seventeen hundred years earlier, was pleased to relate that "the wise man will call a spade a spade."

Backward from there the record tangles. At a far horizon (*circa* B.C. 423) we find a snatch from Aristophanes' *The Clouds:* "That which is a trough he calls a trough." About a century later, according to Plutarch, Philip of Macedon seems to have remembered and embroidered the Greek dramatist's tag. Faced with the complaints of visiting envoys that his troops looked on them as traitors, Philip replied, straight-faced, "The Macedonians are by nature a rough and rustic people who call a tub a tub." Another version quotes Philip: *"Ficus ficus voco, panarium panarium"* ("I call a fig a fig, and a bread dish a bread dish"). Where and how did the spade get into this act, one may ask? Erasmus (1466?–1536), in his *Adagia,* cites Philip as saying: *"Ficus ficus, ligonem ligonem vocat"* ("He calls a fig a fig and a spade a spade"). Trough, tub, and bread dish have enough of a scooped-out shape in common—and spades are scooping tools enough—possibly to have been interchanged in the cliché, and their common Greek root could have caused confusion in translation. Then, too, Erasmus had only to look back to Cicero to feel himself solid in spades.

---

2 In passing, it is thought that a "tinker's dam," for not giving, may have been a worthless bit of clay used to contain a small amount of molten metal until it hardened. What a handy, ready-made euphemism for hypersensitive ears, if true! But who can answer why a "fiddler's bitch" should be the thorough sot that simile asserts she is?

However, the double meaning for fig (for such it seems to be) suggests that Philip of Macedon was well aware of the Mediterranean sexual connotation that comes, as a racy word, through Shakespeare to the present day. Perhaps, in modern idiom, Philip was saying, "We Macedonians know our arses from our elbows, and we call 'em as we see 'em."

Be all that as it may, we welcome you now to the pages of our prospectus. For the fun of it, this has been designed as a sort of guessing game. In each illustration, our invaluable staff artist has captured the essentials of some well-worn phrase. We, in turn, have provided a tag-line by means of clue, and thereafter present, in order, the cliché in approximate modern form and, following this, a selection of earlier and earlier versions. In many cases, we believe we have brought to light the earliest recorded instance but, no doubt, a competent Classicist—or, better, an Assyriologist—could give us cards and spades and still beat us hands down.

Our treasures will be familiar and some, we hope, will be familiar friends. Only a few will prove, like Philip's figs, to have possible roots in the Athenian theater, but, surprisingly, even fewer are products of the last century alone. Among familiar friends, then, we expect that you will find old friends as well.

Who said old friends are best? Francis Bacon (*circa* 1594) credits to an earlier sage—the Spaniard, Alonso of Aragon—the thought: "Age appears to be best in four things—old wood best to burn, old wine to drink, old friends to trust, and old authors to read." But as the searching Burton Stevenson has pointed out, Alonso was long after the holy ben Sira (*circa* B.C. 190) with this truth. In his *Book of Wisdom* is written: "Forsake not an old friend: for the new is not comparable to him: a new friend is as new as new wine; when it is old thou shalt drink it with pleasure."

Joseph W. Valentine
Sherborn, Mass.

LIKE WHOM NO FOOL IS

LIKE WHOM NO FOOL IS

"Old fools is the biggest fools there is."

1876 : Mark Twain, *Tom Sawyer*

"The older a Fool is, the worse he is."

1732 : Thomas Fuller, M.D., *Gnomologia*

"In faith I perceive an olde sawe and a rustic, no foole to the olde foole."

1594 : John Lyly, *Mother Bombie,* Act IV

WHICH THE HAND THAT RULES THE
WORLD ROCKS

WHICH THE HAND THAT RULES THE WORLD ROCKS

"They say that man is mighty,
He governs land and sea,
He wields a mighty scepter,
O'er lesser powers that be;
But a mightier power and stronger
Man from his throne has hurled,
For the hand that rocks the cradle
Is the hand that rules the world."

> 1865 : William Ross Wallace, *What Rules the World* *

* In 1894, William Stewart Ross penned, without credit to Wallace, these unusually parallel lines:

> "They say man rules the universe,
> That subject shore and main
> Kneel down and bless the empery
> Of his majestic reign;
> But a sovereign gentler, mightier,
> Man from this throne has hurled,
> For the hand that rocks the cradle
> Is the hand that rules the world."

FROM WHICH TO BE A CHIP

"She's a chick of the old cock."

> 1678 : Aphra Behn, *Sir Patient Fancy,* Act IV

"Kit after kind. A chip of the old block."

> 1670 : John Ray, *English Proverbs*

"I look upon you as a gem of the old rock."

> 1658 : Sir Thomas Browne, *Hydriotaphia*

"Am I not a child of the same Adam . . . a chip of the same block with him?"

> 1621 : Robert Sanderson, *Sermons*

"Chip of the old flint."

> *circa* B.C. 270 : Theocritus, *Idyls*

THAT ALL WORK AND NO PLAY MAKES
JACK

THAT ALL WORK AND NO PLAY MAKES JACK

"All work and no play makes Jack a dull boy.
All play and no work makes Jack a mere toy."

> 1825 : Maria Edgeworth, *Harry and Lucy*
> *Concluded*

"All work and no play makes Jack a dull boy."

> 1659 : James Howell, *English Proverbs*

"One that reckoneth accounts all the day passeth not an happy moment. One that gladdeneth his heart all the day provideth not for his house. The bowman hitteth the mark, as the steersman reacheth land, by diversity of aim."

> *circa* B.C. 3550 : Ptah-hotep, *Instruction* (Gunn, tr.)

FOR FISH

FOR FISH

"Here's a pretty kettle of fish!"

> 1882 : W. S. Gilbert, *Iolanthe,* Act II

"There'll be a pretty kettle of fish."

> 1850 : Charles Dickens, *David Copperfield*

" 'Here's a pretty kettle of fish,' cries Mrs. Tow-wouse."

> 1742 : Henry Fielding, *Joseph Andrews*

FOR BEING IN THE WIND
THAT BREAKS THE CAMEL'S BACK
AT WHICH A DROWNING MAN WILL
CLUTCH

FOR BEING IN THE WIND

"A straw vote only shows which way the hot air blows."
1907 : O. Henry, "A Ruler of Men"

"Such straws of speech show how blows the wind."
1860 : Charles Reade, *The Cloister and the Hearth*

"Take a straw and throw it up into the Air, you shall see by that which way the wind is."
circa 1654 : John Seldon, *Table-Talk:* "Libels"

THAT BREAKS THE CAMEL'S BACK

"It is the last straw that breaks the camel's back."
1861 : Florence Nightingale, *Notes on Nursing*

"It is the last feather that breaks the horse's back."
1677 : Archbishop John Bramhall, *Works*

"When the cup is brimfull before, the last (though least) super added drop is charged alone to be the cause of all the running over."
1655 : Thomas Fuller, *Church-History of Britain*

"It is not the last drop that empties the water clock, but all that has previously flowed out."
circa 64 A.D. : Seneca, *Ad Lucilium*

AT WHICH A DROWNING MAN WILL CLUTCH

"I cling to you as a drowning man to a straw."
1875 : Robert Louis Stevenson, *Letters*

"Drowning Men will catch at a Rush."
1732 : Thomas Fuller, M.D., *Gnomologia*

"The drowning man snatches at every twig."
1612 : Bishop Joseph Hall, *Contemplations*

FOR HAVING IN ONE'S BELFRY

FOR HAVING IN ONE'S BELFRY

"Sounds like rats in the garret or bats in the belfry." *

1940 : Michael Innes, *Comedy of Errors*

"His father's sister had bats in the belfry."

1926 : Eden Phillpotts, *Peacock House*

"His garret is full of rats."

1910 : O. Henry, "A Little Local Color"

* Burton Stevenson notes (*Home Book of Proverbs, Maxims and Familiar Phrases,* 1959): "The French say, 'Avoir une araignée dans la plafond'—To have a spider in the ceiling."

WHICH MAKE LIGHT WORK

WHICH MAKE LIGHT WORK

"Many hands bring the work quickly to an end."

> 1856 : Charles Cahier, *Quelques Six Mille Proverbes*

"There is no burthen so heavy, which being sustained by many, becometh not light."

> 1574 : Stefano Guazzo, *Civile Conversation*

"ȝit many hondis togider maken liȝt werk."

> 1401 : Friar Daw Topias, *Reply* (to Jack Upland)

"More hands mean more work and more increase."

> *circa* B.C. 800 : Hesiod, *Works and Days*

WHOSE BARK IS WORSE THAN HIS BITE

"His bark was worse than his bite, and he was essentially a kind-hearted man."

1900 : G. C. Broderick, *Memories and Impressions*

"Her new bark is worse than ten times her old bite."

1848 : James Russell Lowell, *A Fable for Critics*

"Monkbarns's bark . . . is muckle waur than his bite."

1816 : Sir Walter Scott, *The Antiquary*

"Presumed to bark the more that he might bite the less."

1655 : Thomas Fuller, *Church-History of Britain*

IN THE EATING OF WHICH IS THE
PROOF

IN THE EATING OF WHICH IS THE PROOF

"The proof of the pudding is in the eating."

1714 : Joseph Addison, *The Spectator*

"All the proof of a pudding is in the eating."

1605 : William Camden, *Remains Concerning Britain*

.

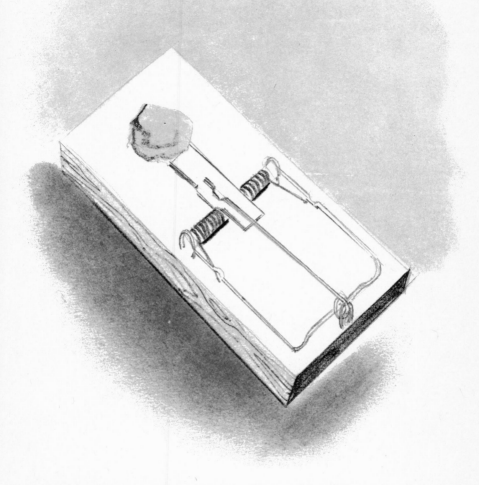

TO THE DOOR OF THE BUILDER OF A
BETTER ONE, THE WORLD WILL BEAT
A PATH

TO THE DOOR OF THE BUILDER OF A BETTER ONE, THE WORLD WILL BEAT A PATH

"If a man can write a better book, preach a better sermon, or make a better mousetrap than his neighbor, though he builds his house in the woods the world will make a beaten path to his door."

> 1871 : Sarah S. B. Yule, *Borrowings* (reported by Mrs. Yule as having been used by Emerson in an address in April, 1871)

"If a man has good corn, or wood, or boards, or pigs, to sell, or can make better chairs or knives, crucibles or church organs, than anybody else, you will find a broad hard-beaten road to his house, though it be in the woods."

> 1855 : Ralph Waldo Emerson, *Journals:* "Common Fame"

"He could invent the best mousetrap."

> 1772 : John Wesley, *Journal*

FOR NOT COUNTING BEFORE THEY'RE
HATCHED

FOR BEING IN EVERY POT

FOR NOT COUNTING BEFORE THEY'RE HATCHED

"We must not reckon our chickens before they are hatched, though they are chipping the shell now."

> 1829 : Sir Walter Scott, *Journal,* 20 May

"Reckon not your Chickens before they are hatch'd. Neither ought we to reckon our Eggs before they are lay'd."

> 1709 : Oswald Dykes, *English Proverbs*

"To swallow gudgeons ere they're catch'd,
And count their chickens ere they're hatch'd."

> 1664 : Samuel Butler, *Hudibras* (Part II)

"He bade me have a care for the future, not to count my chickens before they are hatched."

> *circa* B.C. 570 : Aesop, *Fables:* "The Milkmaid and Her Pail"

FOR BEING IN EVERY POT

"Just consider what a world this would be if ruled by the best thoughts of men of letters! Ignorance would die at once, war would cease, taxation would be lightened, not only every Frenchman, but every man in the world, would have his hen in the pot."

> 1863 : Alexander Smith, *Dreamthorp*

"It is our wish that on Sundays every man will have a chicken in his pot."

> 1598 : Henry IV of France, when he was crowned king

IN WHICH ALL THE EGGS SHOULD NOT BE PUT

IN WHICH ALL THE EGGS SHOULD NOT BE PUT

"Don't venture all your eggs in one basket."

> 1710 : Samuel Palmer, *Moral Essays on Proverbs*

"I must not hang all my bells upon one horse."

> 1659 : James Howell, *English Proverbs*

"I aduentured in one ship to put all my wealth . . . determining either to be a Knight as we saye or a knitter of cappes."

> 1580 : John Lyly, *Euphues and His England*

"Don't risk all your livelihood on the hollow ships."

> *circa* 197 A.D. : Tertullian (quoting a Greek proverb)

FOR KNOWING WHICH SIDE IS
BUTTERED

FOR KNOWING WHICH SIDE IS BUTTERED

"No man knows so well . . . on which side his bread is buttered."

1819 : Sir Walter Scott, *The Bride of Lammermoor*

"Does his Grace think I don't know which side my bread's buttered on?"

1721 : Colley Cibber, *The Refusal,* Act I

"I know upon which syde my bread is buttred."

1546 : John Heywood, *Proverbs*

WHO, WHEN THE CAT'S AWAY, WILL PLAY

WHO, WHEN THE CAT'S AWAY, WILL PLAY

"While the cat runs over the roofs, the mice dance across the floors."

1833 : Honoré de Balzac, *Eugénie Grandet*

"Well kens the mouse when the cat's out o' the house."

1678 : John Ray, *Scottish Proverbs*

"The mowse gth a-brode, wher the cat is not lorde."

circa 1530 : Richard Hill, *Common-place Book*

"The mows lordchypyth [plays the lord] where a cat ys nawt."

circa 1470 : Anonymous, *Harleian MS*

"Sport as you may while the master's away."

circa B.C. 200 : Plautus, *Persa*

IN WHICH TO HAVE ONE FOOT

IN WHICH TO HAVE ONE FOOT

"What, in the devil's name, can you want with a young wife, who have one foot in flannels, and the other in the grave?"

1822 : T. L. Peacock, *Maid Marian*

"What conquest is it to strike him up, who stands but on one leg, and hath the other foot in the grave?"

1642 : Thomas Fuller, *The Holy State*

"Takyng paines to visite him, who hath one of his feet alreadie within the graue, and the other stepping after with conuenient speede."

1566 : William Painter, *The Pallace of Pleasure*

"An old dotard with one foot already in the grave."

circa 95 A.D. : Plutarch, *Moralia:* "Education of Children"

THAN WHICH TWO HEADS ARE
BETTER

FOR BEING SCREWED ON THE RIGHT
WAY

FOR HAVING ABOVE WATER

THAN WHICH TWO HEADS ARE BETTER

"Two Heads are better than one, quoth the Woman, when she had her dog with her to the Market."

> 1732 : Thomas Fuller, M.D., *Gnomologia*

"This olde sayinge, Twoe wytts (or moe) to bee better then one."

> 1558 : Sir William Forrest, *The Second Gresield*

"Two han more wit then on."

> *circa* 1390 : John Gower, *Confessio Amantis*

"When two go together, one discerneth before the other how profit may be had; whereas if one alone perceive aught, yet is his wit the shorter, and but slender his device."

> *circa* B.C. 850 : Homer, *Iliad*

FOR BEING SCREWED ON THE RIGHT WAY

"The father . . . had a . . . contempt for those without force of character or capacity . . . who . . . had not 'their head screwed on the right way.' "

> 1843 : Mandell Creighton, *Life and Letters*

FOR HAVING ABOVE WATER

"I'm . . . just able by the greatest caution and prudence to keep my head above water."

> 1860 : R. S. Surtees, *Plain or Ring?*

"If I can hold my head above water, it is all I can."

> 1742 : Henry Fielding, *Joseph Andrews*

"Scarce their heads above ground they could keep."

> 1627 : Michael Drayton, *Moon-Calf*

FOR BEING AS THE TWIG
IS BENT

FOR BEING AS THE TWIG IS BENT

"As the twig is bent, the tree's inclined."

> 1732 : Alexander Pope, "Moral Essays"

"Best to bend while 'tis a twig."

> 1670 : John Ray, *English Proverbs*

"Thraw the rod while it is green."

> 1641 : David Fergusson, *Scottish Proverbs*

"As longe as the twygge is gentell and plyent . . . With small force and strength it may be bent."

> *circa* 1560 : Thomas Ingelend, *The Disobedient Child*

WHO CAN'T BE TAUGHT NEW TRICKS

WHO CAN'T BE TAUGHT NEW TRICKS

"Can't learn an old dog new tricks."

> 1876 : Mark Twain, *Tom Sawyer*

"I am ower auld a dog to learn new tricks."

> 1819 : Sir Walter Scott, *The Bride of Lammermoor*

"An old dog will learn no tricks. It's all one to physic the dead, as to instruct old men."

> 1670 : John Ray, *English Proverbs*

"It is hard to teach an old dog new tricks."

> 1605 : William Camden, *Remains Concerning Britain*

"The dogge must lerne it when he is a whelpe, or els it wyl not be; for it is harde to make an olde dogge stoupe."

> 1523 : Sir Anthony Fitzherbert, *The Boke of Husbandrye*

FOR THROWING IN THE WORKS

FOR THROWING IN THE WORKS

"Don't throw a monkey-wrench into the machinery!"

> 1920 : Philander Johnson, "Shooting Stars"
> (*Everybody's Magazine,* May)

"I may not know anything about my own machinery, but I know how to stick a ramrod into the other fellow's."

> 1913 : Shaw, *Heartbreak House*

FOR SPARING THE ROD AND SPOILING

FOR SPARING THE ROD AND SPOILING

"Spare the Rod, and spoil the Child."

> 1732 : Thomas Fuller, M.D., *Gnomologia*

"He that sparith the zerde, hatith his sone."

> 1382 : John Wycliffe, *Proverbs*

"Who-so spareth the sprynge spilleth his children."

> 1377 : William Langland, *Piers Plowman*

"Se ðe sparað his zyrde, he hata ð his cild."

> *circa* 995 : Aelfric, *Homilies* (II)

"He that spareth his rod hateth his son but he that loveth him chasteneth him betimes."

> *circa* B.C. 1000 : Proverbs 13:24

FOR NO PLACE TO BE LIKE
FOR BEING A MAN'S CASTLE
WHICH IT TAKES A HEAP O' LIVING
TO MAKE A HOUSE

FOR NO PLACE TO BE LIKE

" 'Mid pleasures and palaces though we may roam,
Be it ever so humble, there's no place like home."

> 1823 : John Howard Payne, "Home, Sweet Home,"
> from the opera *Clari, The Maid of Milan*

"For home though homely twere, yet it is sweet."

> 1591 : Sir John Harington, tr., *Orlando Furioso*

"No place is more delightful than one's own fireside."

> B.C. 46 : Cicero, *Ad Familiares*

FOR BEING A MAN'S CASTLE

"My houfe is my caftle, gentlemen, and nobody muft offer
violence here."

> 1767 : Arthur Murphy, *School for Guardians*,
> Act V

"A man's house is his castle. This is a kind of law proverb; Jura
publica favent privato domus."

> 1678 : John Ray, *English Proverbs* (additions)

"Ma meason est à moy come mon castel."

> 1567 : Sir William Stanford, *Les Plees del Coron*

WHICH IT TAKES A HEAP O' LIVING TO MAKE A HOUSE

"To begin with, it takes a heap o' payin'."

> 1935 : Ogden Nash, "A Heap o' Livin' "

"It takes a heap o' livin' in a house t' make it home."

> 1916 : Edgar A. Guest, "Home"

WHO FROM HIS MONEY IS SOON
PARTED

WHO FROM HIS MONEY IS SOON PARTED

"Fools and their money are soon parted."

> 1748 : Tobias Smollett, *Roderick Random*

"A foole oft finds himselfe short of his reckonings."

> 1611 : Randle Cotgrave, *Dictionary:* Fol

"A foole and his monie be soone at debate.
Which after with sorrow repents him too late."

> 1573 : Thomas Tusser, *Fiue Hundreth Pointes of Good Husbandrie*

FOR FEATHERING ONE'S OWN
FOR FOULING ONE'S OWN

FOR FEATHERING ONE'S OWN

"Mr. Badman had well feathered his Nest with other men's goods and money."

> 1680 : John Bunyan, *Pilgrim's Progress* (Part I)

"Thou hast fethred thy nest, and hast crowns in thy purse."

> 1590 : Robert Greene, *Works*

"Nowe ys the tyme come . . . to make vp my mouth, and to feather my neste."

> 1553 : Anonymous, *Respublica*, Act I

FOR FOULING ONE'S OWN

"What's the use o' vilifying ane's country? . . . It's an ill bird that files its ain nest."

> 1818 : Sir Walter Scott, *Rob Roy*

"An olde proverbe seyde ys in englyssh: men seyn 'that brid or foule ys dyshonest, what that he be and holden ful chirlyssh, that vseth to defoule his oone neste.' "

> 1402 : Thomas Hoccleve, *Minor Poems*

"Only foul birds soil their own nests."

> *circa* 1023 : Egbert Lüttich, *Fecunda Ratis*

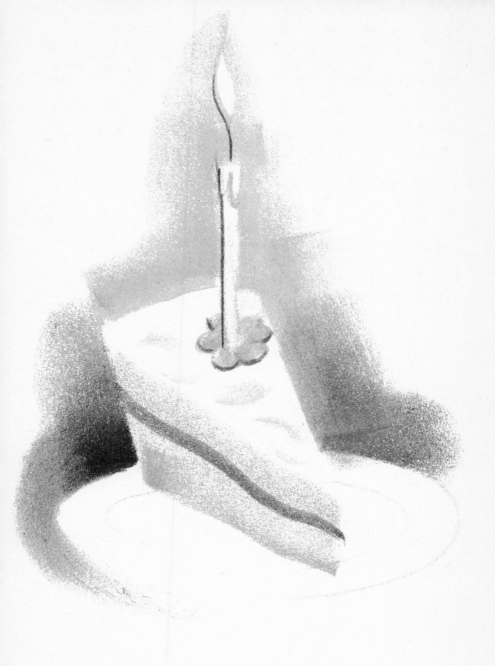

THAT CANNOT BE HAD AND EATEN

THAT CANNOT BE HAD AND EATEN

"One cannot eat one's cake and have it too."

> 1880 : T. H. Huxley, in a letter to Herbert
> Spencer, 27 December

"She was handsome in her time; but she cannot eat her cake and have her cake."

> 1738 : Jonathan Swift, *Polite Conversation:*
> Dialogue I

"Lay out thy joy, yet hope to save it?
Wouldst thou both eat thy cake, and have it?"

> *circa* 1633 : George Herbert, "The Size"

"Wolde you bothe eate your cake, and haue your cake?"

> 1546 : John Heywood, *Proverbs*

FOR BEING WITHIN WHEELS

FOR BEING WITHIN WHEELS

" 'And a bird-cage, sir,' said Sam. 'Veels within veels, a prison in a prison.' "

1837 : Charles Dickens, *Pickwick Papers*

"As a wheel within a wheel."

1709 : Bernard Mandeville, *The Virgin Unmask'd*

". . . their appearance and their work was as it were a wheel in the middle of a wheel."

circa B.C. 600 : Ezekiel 1:16

FOR NOT CASTING PEARLS BEFORE

FOR NOT CASTING PEARLS BEFORE

"Oh, I do a thankless thing, and cast pearls before swine."

1848 : Charles Dickens, *Dombey and Son*

"For to caft Eloquence amongft a companie of Stinctards, is all one as if a man fhould fcatter Pearle amongft the hoggifh animals ecliped Swine."

1606 : John Day, *The Ile of Gvls,* Act IV

"Men should not put . . . perles whight,
To-fore rude swyne."

circa 1430 : John Lydgate, *Minor Poems*

"Neither cast ye your pearls before swine, lest they trample them under their feet, and turn again and rend you."

circa 50 A.D. : Matthew 7:6

FOR PUTTING BEFORE THE HORSE

FOR PUTTING BEFORE THE HORSE

"Having, as usual, set the cart before the horse, and taken the effect for the cause."

1863 : Charles Kingsley, *The Water Babies*

"Muche like as if we woulde go make the carte to drawe the horse."

1528 : Sir Thomas More, *Works*

"Moche uolk of religion zetteþ þe zuolz be-uore þe oksen."

1340 : Dan Michel, *Ayenbite of Inwyt*

"I'll put my cart before the horse, like Homer."

B.C. 61 : Cicero, *Ad Atticum*

"The hind hunts the dogs."

circa B.C. 270 : Theocritus, *Idyls*

FOR BEING WHERE SMOKE IS

FOR BEING INTO OUT OF THE
FRYING PAN

IN WHICH TO HAVE MORE THAN
ONE IRON

FOR BEING WHERE SMOKE IS

"There is no fire but there will be some smoak."

1650 : Thomas Hubbert, A Pill to Purge Formality

". . . that, where greet fyr hath longe tyme endured, that ther ne dwellth som vapour of warmnesse."

circa 1386 : Geoffrey Chaucer, Canterbury Tales: "The Tale of Melibeus"

"Nor, when a fire is made, will smoke be lacking."

circa B.C. 43 : Publilius Syrus, Sententiae

FOR BEING INTO OUT OF THE FRYING PAN

"It is a sad choice, Frying or Fire."

1732 : Thomas Fuller, M.D., Gnomologia

"Some of the ditch shy are, yet can
Lie tumbling in the mire:
Some, though they shun the frying-pan,
Do leap into the fire."

1684 : John Bunyan, Pilgrim's Progress (Part II)

"From syspicion to knowlage of yll, forsoothe,
Could make ye dooe, but as the flounder doothe,
Leape out of the friyng pan into the fyre,
And chaunge from yll peyn to wurs is worth small hyre."

1546 : John Heywood, Proverbs

IN WHICH TO HAVE MORE THAN ONE IRON

"I had now several important irons in the fire, and all to be struck whilst hot."

1751 : Robert Pollock, Peter Wilkins

"Mony yrons in the fire part mon coole."

1641 : David Fergusson, Scottish Proverbs

"Put no more so many yrons in the fyre at ones."

1549 : Sir William Paget, in a letter to Somerset, 7 July

FOR A MIND TO HAVE
TO HAVE THE INSIDE
TO BE ON THE RIGHT

FOR A MIND TO HAVE

"I have a single-track mind."

> 1917 : Woodrow Wilson, in a speech at the
> National Press Club, Washington, D.C.

TO HAVE THE INSIDE

"When a woman . . . has the inside track . . . the man has no show whatever."

> 1914 : Gertrude Atherton, *Perch of the Devil*

"I guess I've got the inside track."

> 1885 : William Dean Howells, *The Rise of Silas Lapham*

"The railroad from Omaha appears to have . . . the inside track."

> 1867 : J. F. Meline, *Sainte Fe and Back*

TO BE ON THE RIGHT

"You're on the right track."

> *circa* B.C. 200 : Plautus, *Asinaria*

THAT DOESN'T MAKE A SUMMER

THAT DOESN'T MAKE A SUMMER

"One swallow makes not a spring, nor one woodcock a winter."

1678 : John Ray, *English Proverbs* (additions)

"Nay, soft (said the widow) one swallow makes not a summer, nor one meeting a marriage."

1597 : Thomas Deloney, *Jacke of Newbery*

"One faire day assureth not a good Sommer, nor one flying Swalow prognosticateth not a good yere."

1548 : Edward Hall, *Chronicle*

"One swallow does not make spring, nor does one fine day."

circa B.C. 335 : Aristotle, *Nicomachean Ethics*

FOR READING BETWEEN

FOR READING BETWEEN

"One method of cryptography is to write so that the hidden message is revealed only when alternate lines are read. Thus lines 2, 4, 6 of the following cryptogram would convey the warning to Lord Montagle of the Gunpowder Plot.

'My lord, having just returned from Paris
2   stay away from the house tonight
and give me the pleasure of your company,
4   for God and man have concurred to punish
those who pay not regard to their health, and
6   the wickedness of the time
adds greatly to its wear and tear.' "

1870 : E. Cobham Brewer, *A Dictionary of Phrase and Fable*

Another, even simpler, method involves the use of "invisible inks," actually writing the hidden message in the blank space between the lines of the false message. This technique—of unknown antiquity—can scarcely have antedated the use of inks, being useless with clay tablets or stone inscriptions, and therefore could be as old as Egyptian papyrus (*circa* B.C. 3000). Ed. note.

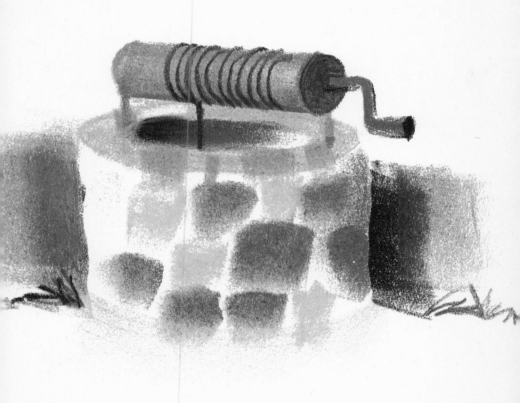

FROM WHICH, UNTIL IT RUNS DRY, THE
WATER IS NEVER MISSED

FROM WHICH, UNTIL IT RUNS DRY, THE WATER IS NEVER MISSED

"Has it not been dinned into us by proverb and sermon and fable that we never miss the music till the sweet-voiced bird has flown?"

> 1907 : O. Henry, "The Pendulum"

"You Never Miss the Water Till the Well Runs Dry"

> 1876 : Anonymous song, an American minstrel favorite for many years

"When the well's dry, we know the worth of water."

> 1746 : Benjamin Franklin, *Poor Richard's Almanack*

"It's when they miss the lamp men pour in oil."

> *circa* B.C. 430 : Anaxagoras to Pericles

WHICH SPOILS THE BARREL

WHICH SPOILS THE BARREL

"The rotten apple spoils his companions."

> 1736 : Benjamin Franklin, *Poor Richard's Almanack*

"One scabbed sheep infecteth all the fold."

> *circa* 1530 : Richard Hill, *Common-place Book*

"Wel bet is roten appel out of hord
Than it rotie al the remenaunt."

> *circa* 1386 : Geoffrey Chaucer, *Canterbury Tales:* "The Cook's Tale"

"A roted eppel amang þe holen, makeþ rotie þe y-zounde."

> 1340 : Dan Michel, *Ayenbite of Inwyt*

WHICH IS BETTER THAN NONE

WHICH IS BETTER THAN NONE

"We must live somehow, and half a loaf is better than no bread."

> 1850 : Charles Kingsley, *Alton Locke*

"He is a foole who counts not halfe a loafe better then no bread, or despiseth the moonshine because the sunne is down."

> 1642 : Daniel Rogers, *Naaman the Syrian:* To the Reader

"Better a louse in the pot than no flesh at all."

> 1605 : William Camden, *Remains Concerning Britain*

"Throw no gyft agayne at the geuers head;
For better is halfe a lofe than no bread."

> 1546 : John Heywood, *Proverbs*

LIKE WHICH TO SLEEP

FOR THINGS TO BE AS EASY AS
ROLLING OFF

ON WHICH TO SIT LIKE A BUMP

LIKE WHICH TO SLEEP

"You sleep like a log."

> 1943 : John Lodwick, *Running to Paradise*

"I shall sleep like a top."

> 1668 : Sir William Davenant, *Rivals,* Act III

"He sleep as a swyn."

> *circa* 1386 : Geoffrey Chaucer, *Canterbury Tales:*
> "Man of Law's Tale"

FOR THINGS TO BE AS EASY AS ROLLING OFF

"I could do it as easy as rolling off a log."

> 1889 : Mark Twain, *A Connecticut Yankee*

"He gradually went away from the Lubber, and won the heat 'just as easy as rolling off a log.' "

> 1839 : New Orleans *Picayune*

ON WHICH TO SIT LIKE A BUMP

"Ye aint goin' to set there like a bump on a log 'thought sayin' a word ter pay for yer vittles, air ye?"

> 1889 : Kate Douglas Wiggin, *The Birds' Christmas Carol*

WHICH RATS DESERT

WHICH RATS DESERT

"A rotten carcass of a boat . . . the very rats
Instinctively have quit it."

> 1611 : Shakespeare, *The Tempest,* Act I

"It is the Wisdome of Rats that will be sure to leaue a **House,**
somewhat before it fall."

> 1597 : Francis Bacon, *Essays:* "Of Wisdome **for a**
> Man's Self"

"Rats and dormice will forsake old and ruinous houses, three
months before they fall."

> *circa* 1580 : Thomas Lupton, *A Thousand Notable*
> *Things of Sundrie Sorts*

FOR LOCKING AFTER THE HORSE IS
STOLEN

FOR LOCKING AFTER THE HORSE IS STOLEN

"It was only shutting the Stable Door after the Stead was stoln."

> 1719 : Daniel Defoe, *Robinson Crusoe*

"When the daughter is stolen, shut Pepper-gate."

> 1662 : Thomas Fuller, *The History of the Worthies of England:* "Chester." [Stevenson (1959) notes Fuller's explanation "that Pepper-gate was a postern in the wall surrounding the city of Chester, through which a mayor's daughter had eloped, and which he thereupon caused to be bricked up."]

"When steedes are stolne tys bootles doores to barre."

> 1587 : George Turberville, *Tragical Tales*

"Whan the stede is stolyn to shyt the stable dore Comys small pleasoure profyte or vauntage."

> 1508 : Alexander Barclay, *The Shyp of Folys*

"When the hors is stole steke the stabull-dore."

> *circa* 1350 : Anonymous, *Douce MS*

"Country folk have a saying: Too late to close the stable when the horse is lost."

> *circa* 1190 : Anonymous, *Li Proverb au Vilain*

FOR NOT LOOKING IN THE MOUTH

FOR NOT LOOKING IN THE MOUTH

"I thought I was not to look a gift-horse in the mouth, sir."

1871 : George Eliot, *Middlemarch*

"Where gyftis be geuen freely, est west north or south,
No man ought to looke a geuen hors in the mouth."

1546 : John Heywood, *Proverbs*

"A gyuen hors may not be loked in the tethe."

circa 1520 : John Stanbridge, *Vulgaria*

"Do not—as the common proverb has it—scrutinize the teeth of
a gift horse."

circa 400 A.D. : Saint Jerome, *Commentary on the
Epistle to the Ephesians*

WHO CAN'T BE CHOOSERS
WHO, IF WISHES WERE HORSES,
WOULD BE RIDING

WHO CAN'T BE CHOOSERS

"Beggars mustn't be choosers."

> 1857 : Anthony Trollope, *Barchester Towers*

"My lord, says I, beggars must not be choosers."

> *circa* 1726 : Sir John Vanbrugh, *Journey to London*, Act III

"Nay (quoth I) be they wynners or loosers,
Folke saie alwaie, beggars should be no choosers."

> 1546 : John Heywood, *Proverbs*

WHO, IF WISHES WERE HORSES, WOULD RIDE

"If wishes were horses, beggars wad ride,
And a' the warld be drowned in pride."

> 1862 : A. Hislop, *Proverbs of Scotland*

"If wishes were horses, Beggars would ride,
If turnips were watches, I'd wear one at my side."

> 1844 : H. O. Halliwell, *Nursery Rhymes of England*

"If wishes were horses, beggars would ride."

> 1721 : James Kelly, *Scottish Proverbs*

"If wishes were Thrushes, then beggars would eat birds."

> 1670 : John Ray, *English Proverbs*

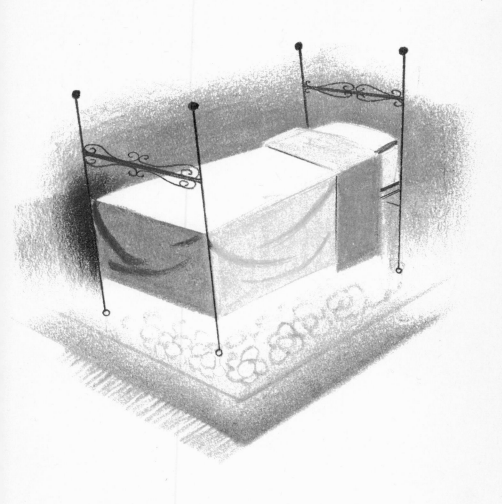

OF ONE'S OWN MAKING, FOR NOW
LYING IN

OF ONE'S OWN MAKING, FOR NOW LYING IN

"As he has made his bed, so he must lie upon it."

1857 : Anthony Trollope, *Barchester Towers*

"He that makes his Bed ill, must be contented to lie ill."

1732 : Thomas Fuller, M.D., *Gnomologia*

"He that makes his bed ill, lies there."

1651 : George Herbert, *Jacula Prudentum*

"Lett them . . . go to there bedd, as themselves shall make it."

circa 1590 : Gabriel Harvey, *Marginalia*

WHICH IF ROLLING GATHER NO MOSS
FOR PEOPLE WHO LIVE IN GLASS
HOUSES NOT TO THROW

WHICH IF ROLLING GATHER NO MOSS

"We keep repeating the silly proverb that rolling stones gather no moss, as if moss were a desirable parasite."

> 1914 : Shaw, *Misalliance:* Preface

"Selden Moseth the Merbelston that men ofte treden."

> 1377 : William Langland, *Piers Plowman*

"Grass grows not upon revolving stones."

> 1257 : Saadi, *Būstān*

FOR PEOPLE WHO LIVE IN GLASS HOUSES NOT TO THROW

"They who live in glass houses should not throw stones."

> 1855 : H. G. Bohn, *Handbook of Proverbs*

"Steenie, Steenie, those who live in glass houses should be carefu' how they fling stanes."

> circa 1604 : James I of England, to the Duke of Buckingham

"And for-thy, who that hath a hed of verre,
For cast of stones war him in the werre!"

> 1374 : Geoffrey Chaucer, "Troilus and Criseyde"

AT WHOM LOVE LAUGHS

AT WHOM LOVE LAUGHS

"Dorothy . . . was kept almost a prisoner. . . . Love, however, laughs at locksmiths."

1877 : Edward Walford, *Tales of Our Great Families*

"Were beauty under twenty locks kept fast,
Yet love breaks through and picks them all at last."

1593 : Shakespeare, *Venus and Adonis*

FOR NOT CHANGING IN MIDSTREAM

FOR NOT CHANGING IN MIDSTREAM

"I do not allow myself to suppose that either the convention or the League have concluded to decide that I am either the greatest or the best man in America, but rather they have concluded that it is not best to swap horses while crossing the river, and have further concluded that I am not so poor a horse that they might not make a botch of it trying to swap."

> 1864 : Abraham Lincoln, speech of reply to the National Union League

"I have not permitted myself, gentlemen, to conclude that I am the best man in the country, but I am reminded in this connection of an old Dutch farmer who remarked that it was not best to swap horses while crossing a stream."

> (W. O. Stoddard's version of the same speech)

FOR HASTE TO MAKE

FOR HASTE TO MAKE

"Haste makes waste, and waste makes want, and want makes strife between the goodman and his wife."

> 1678 : John Ray, *English Proverbs* (additions)

"Festina lente, Not too fast;
For haste (the proverb says) makes waste."

> 1663 : Samuel Butler, *Hudibras* (Part I)

"It is good that men looke before they leape, hast makes wast."

> *circa* 1591 : Henry Smith, *Sermons*

"In wikked haste is no profit."

> *circa* 1386 : Geoffrey Chaucer, *Canterbury Tales:* "The Tale of Melibeus"

THE SAUCE FOR WHICH IS SAUCE FOR THE GANDER

THE SAUCE FOR WHICH IS SAUCE FOR THE GANDER

"(Miss gives Neverout a smart pinch) . . . Neverout: (giving Miss a pinch) 'Take that, miss; what's sauce for a goose is sauce for a gander.' "

> 1738 : Jonathan Swift, *Polite Conversation:*
> Dialogue II

"That that's good sawce for a goose, is good for a gander."

> 1670 : John Ray, *English Proverbs*

"As well for the coowe calf as for the bull."

> 1546 : John Heywood, *Proverbs*

"The same for Attius as for Tettius."

> *circa* B.C. 50 : Marcus Varro, *Testamentum*

TO BE LEFT HOLDING
OUT OF WHICH THE CAT IS LET

TO BE LEFT HOLDING

"We're going to let you hold the bag."

> 1924 : Laurence Stallings and Maxwell Anderson,
> *What Price Glory?*, Act I

"She gave me the bag to hold, and was smuggling in a corner with a rich old Puritan."

> 1823 : Sir Walter Scott, *Peveril of the Peak*

"She will leave Spain the bag to hold."

> 1793 : Thomas Jefferson, *Writings*

OUT OF WHICH THE CAT IS LET

"The cat's out of the bag." *

> 1910 : Shaw, *Misalliance*

"He was afraid, being a little affected with wine, [he] would 'let the cat out of the bag.' "

> 1836 : Frederick Marryat, *Midshipman Easy*

"I forgot, I was nigh letting the cat out of the bag again."

> 1796 : Maria Edgeworth, *The Parent's Assistant*

---

* E. Cobham Brewer notes (1870): "It was formerly a trick among country folk to substitute a cat for a sucking-pig, and bring it in a bag to market. If any greenhorn chose to buy 'a pig in a poke' without examination, all very well; but if he opened the sack, 'he let the cat out of the bag,' and the trick was disclosed."

FOR TAKING BY THE HORNS

FOR TAKING BY THE HORNS

"I have often been told to be bold, and take the bull by the horns."

> 1869 : C. H. Spurgeon, *John Ploughman's Talk*

"He took the bull fairly by the horns."

> 1849 : Lord Lytton, *The Caxtons*

"He had not, as the phrase goes, taken the bull by the horns."

> 1816 : Sir Walter Scott, *Old Mortality*

"Take a bull by the horn and a man by his word."

> 1659 : James Howell, *English Proverbs*

"An ox is taken by the horns, and a man by the tongue."

> 1651 : George Herbert, *Jacula Prudentum*

BEFORE WHICH THE DARKEST HOUR
COMES

BEFORE WHICH THE DARKEST HOUR COMES

"The darkest hour precedes the dawn."

> 1880 : Benjamin Disraeli, *Endymion*

"This is a terrible hour, but it is often that darkest point which precedes the rise of day."

> 1849 : Charlotte Brontë, *Shirley*

"It is always darkest just before the day dawneth."

> 1650 : Thomas Fuller, *A Pisgah-Sight of Palestine*

"Nay, misery's blackest night may chance, by Fortune's turn, to show a happy dawn."

> *circa* B.C. 414 : Euripides, *Iphigenia in Tauris*

AT WHOM A CAT MAY LOOK
WHO IS EVERY INCH

AT WHOM A CAT MAY LOOK

"A Cat may look at a King. This is a saucy Proverb, generally made use of by pragmatical Persons."

> 1730 : Nathan Bailey, *Dictionary:* Cat

"A bawbee cat may look at a King."

> 1678 : John Ray, *Scottish Proverbs*

"A Cat may look at a King, and a swaines eye hath as high a reach as a Lords looke."

> 1590 : Robert Greene, *Never Too Late*

"A cat maie looke on a king, ye know."

> 1546 : John Heywood, *Proverbs*

WHO IS EVERY INCH

"He's a man every inch of him . . ."

> 1892 : William E. Henley and Robert Louis Stevenson, *Admiral Guinea*

"A king so good, so just, so great,
That at his birth the heavenly council paused
And then at last cried out, This is a man!"

> 1682 : John Dryden, *The Duke of Guise,* Act I

"A man every inch of him."

> 1678 : John Ray, *English Proverbs* (additions)

"Ay, every inch a King."

> 1605 : Shakespeare, *King Lear,* Act IV

FOR GOING MORE EASILY THROUGH
THE NEEDLE'S EYE

FOR GOING MORE EASILY THROUGH THE NEEDLE'S EYE

"It is as hard to come as for a camel to thread the postern of a small needle's eye."

1595 : Shakespeare, Richard II, Act V

"It is easier for a camel to go through the eye of a needle, than for a rich man to enter into the kingdom of God."

circa 65 A.D. : Matthew 19:24 *

---

* Burton Stevenson (1959) notes: "This is a paraphrase of a proverb which is common in various forms throughout the East—in fact in all countries familiar with the camel: 'To let a camel go through the hole of a needle' (Hebrew); 'A camel's head will not pass through the eye of a needle' (Osmanli); 'Can a camel pass through the eye of a needle?' (Tamil), and so on."

AMONG WHOM THERE IS HONOR
OF WHOM ONE IS SET TO CATCH
ANOTHER

AMONG WHOM THERE IS HONOR

"Thieves make a point of honor . . . of being honest to one another."

1721 : Daniel Defoe, History of Colonel Jack

"A plague upon it when thieves cannot be true one to another."

1597 : Shakespeare, Henry IV, Act II

"Furthermore, they say that even thieves have a code of laws to heed and submit to."

circa B.C. 45 : Cicero, De Officiis (Book II)

OF WHOM ONE IS SET TO CATCH ANOTHER

" 'You have been all your life evading the laws . . . do you think this has qualified you peculiarly for being a guardian of the laws?' Sir Terence replied, 'Yes, sure; set a thief to catch a thief is no bad maxim.' "

1812 : Maria Edgeworth, Absentee

"One thief knoweth another."

1633 : Thomas Draxe, Biblioteca

"A thief myself, I know the tracks of a thief."

circa B.C. 250 : Callimachus, Epigrams

THAT ONE IN THE HAND IS WORTH

THAT ONE IN THE HAND IS WORTH

"One bird in the hand is worth two in the bush."

> 1709 : Oswald Dykes, *English Proverbs*

"Better one byrde in hande than ten in the wood."

> 1546 : John Heywood, *Proverbs*

"Betyr ys a byrd in the hond than tweye in the wode."

> *circa* 1470 : Anonymous, *Harleian MS*

"I should be foolish to release the bird I have in my hand, in order to pursue another."

> *circa* B.C. 570 : Aesop, *Fables:* "The Nightingale and the Hawk"

FOR JUMPING ON

FOR JUMPING ON

"Many of those Democrats . . . who rushed into the Bryan band-wagon . . . will now be seen crawling out over the tail-board."

1906 : N.Y. Evening Post, 5 September

"It is a lamentable fact that . . . our commercial enemy . . . should come along with a band wagon loaded with hobgoblins."

1893 : Congressional Record

FOR CALLING A SPADE

FOR CALLING A SPADE

"I love to call a spade a spade."

> 1738 : Jonathan Swift, *Polite Conversation:*
> Dialogue III

"I think it good plain English, without fraud,
To call a spade a spade, a bawd a bawd."

> 1619 : John Taylor, "A Kicksy Winsey"

"Brought up like a rude Macedon, and taught to call a spade a spade."

> 1579 : Stephen Gosson, *Ephemerides*

"Confutation is my name, the friend of truth and candor . . . I call a fig a fig, a tub a tub."

> *circa* B.C. 300 : Menander, *Fragments*

"The Macedonians are by nature a rough and rustic people who call a tub a tub."

> *circa* B.C. 350 : Philip of Macedon, as given by
> Plutarch, *Sayings of Kings and Commanders*

"That which is a trough he calls a trough."

> *circa* B.C. 423 : Aristophanes, *The Clouds*

WHO SPOIL THE BROTH

"The more Cooks, the worse Broth."

> 1732 : Thomas Fuller, M.D., *Gnomologia*

"There is the proverb, the more cooks the worse pottage."

> 1575 : George Gascoigne, *Life of Carew*

"Too many generals lost Caria."

> *circa* 125 A.D. : Diogenianus, *Adagia*

FOR HAVING BY THE TAIL

FOR HAVING BY THE TAIL

"When you've got an elephant by the hind leg, and he's trying
to run away, it's best to let him run."

> 1865 : Abraham Lincoln, remark to Charles A.
> Dana a few hours before his (Lincoln's)
> assassination

"You dare as well take a Bear by the Tooth,
That is, You dare not attempt it."

> 1736 : Nathan Bailey, *Dictionary:* Bear

"To . . . take the beare by the tooth."

> 1601 : Arthur Dent, *Pathway to Heauen*

WHICH ONE MAN'S MEAT IS ANOTHER MAN'S

WHICH ONE MAN'S MEAT IS ANOTHER MAN'S

"Is it not even a proverb, that what is meat to one man is poison to another?"

circa 1720 : Matthew Prior, *Dialogues of the Dead*

"As concerning the hatred of princes, one mans meate is another mans poyson."

1614 : William Barclay, *Nepenthes or the Vertues of Tobacco*

"Ofte thinge that is holsome and good to men is poyson to other bestes."

1398 : John de Trevisa, tr., *De Proprietatibus Rerum*

"What to one man is food, to another is rank poison."

B.C. 45 : Lucretius, *De Rerum Natura*

FOR BARKING UP

FOR BARKING UP

"If my coon dog does sometimes bark up the wrong tree, he don't mean any harm by it."

1866 : C. H. Smith, *Bill Arp*

"I told him . . . that he reminded me of the meanest thing on God's earth, an old coon dog, barking up the wrong tree."

1833 : David Crockett, *Sketches*

"You are barking up the wrong tree, Johnson."

1832 : James Hall, *Legends of the West*

CREDIT WHERE CREDIT IS DUE

The entire curatorial staff of the Cliché Museum-to-be—an unwieldy group at best—acknowledges that its task would have been impossible without the aid and comfort afforded by all their fellow workers in this field.

To give some substance to their appreciation of this indebtedness, the curators have—in many cases with unparalleled retro-activity—unanimously (and unilaterally) appointed a number of the most ardent scholars to the following honorary posts:

CHIEF CURATOR EMERITUS

Burton Stevenson

CURATORS EMERITUS

Henry L. Mencken
John Bartlett
Rev. E. Cobham Brewer
Dr. Thomas Fuller
Rev. Thomas Fuller
John Ray
George Herbert
John Heywood

CURATORS *NOLI VOLI*

Charles E. Funk
Eric Partridge
Selwyn G. Champion
Mitford M. Matthews

The author—despite savage backbiting—would feel things sadly awry if he did not simultaneously give commendation to Margaret Purcell, Betty Valentine, and their assorted progeny for their forbearance, as well as their untiring help or hindrance as the case may be.